INSIDE MLS

REAL SALT LAKE

BY SAM MOUSSAVI

SportsZone
An Imprint of Abdo Publishing
abdobooks.com

abdobooks.com

Published by Abdo Publishing, a division of ABDO, PO Box 398166, Minneapolis, Minnesota 55439. Copyright © 2022 by Abdo Consulting Group, Inc. International copyrights reserved in all countries. No part of this book may be reproduced in any form without written permission from the publisher. SportsZone™ is a trademark and logo of Abdo Publishing.

Printed in the United States of America, North Mankato, Minnesota
052021
092021

Cover Photo: Maria Lysaker/Cal Sport Media/AP Images
Interior Photos: George Frey/AP Images, 4–5; Mark J. Terrill/AP Images, 7; Melissa Majchrzak/Major League Soccer/Getty Images, 9; Jim Prisching/AP Images, 11; Elaine Thompson/AP Images, 13, 35, 37; Douglas C. Pizac/AP Images, 15, 16; Dustin Bradford/Icon SMI/Newscom, 19; John Smierciak/AP Images, 21; Francisco Kjolseth/Salt Lake Tribune/AP Images, 23; Andy Mead/Icon SMI/Newscom, 25, 29; Ted S. Warren/AP Images, 26; Dorn Byg/Cal Sport Media/AP Images, 30; Luis M. Alvarez/AP Images, 33; George Frey/Getty Images Sport/Getty Images, 38; Leah Hogsten/Salt Lake Tribune/AP Images, 41; Colin E. Braley/AP Images, 42

Editor: Patrick Donnelly
Series Designer: Dan Peluso

Library of Congress Control Number: 2020948224

Publisher's Cataloging-in-Publication Data

Names: Moussavi, Sam, author.
Title: Real Salt Lake / by Sam Moussavi
Description: Minneapolis, Minnesota : Abdo Publishing, 2022 | Series: Inside MLS | Includes online resources and index.
Identifiers: ISBN 9781532194818 (lib. bdg.) | ISBN 9781098214470 (ebook)
Subjects: LCSH: Real Salt Lake (Soccer team)--Juvenile literature. | Soccer teams--Juvenile literature. | Professional sports franchises--Juvenile literature. | Sports Teams--Juvenile literature.
Classification: DDC 796.334--dc23

TABLE OF **CONTENTS**

CHAPTER 1
AN IMPROBABLE RUN............... 4

CHAPTER 2
CLUB MILESTONES................ 14

CHAPTER 3
STARS OF SALT LAKE............. 24

CHAPTER 4
***REAL* BIG MOMENTS**............... 34

TIMELINE	44
TEAM FACTS	45
GLOSSARY	46
MORE INFORMATION	47
ONLINE RESOURCES	47
INDEX	48
ABOUT THE AUTHOR	48

CHAPTER 1

AN IMPROBABLE
RUN

Real Salt Lake entered 2009 with high expectations. The club was coming off the best of its four seasons in Major League Soccer (MLS). RSL—as the club is commonly known—had finished seventh in the league in 2008. Then it reached the conference finals before falling to the New York Red Bulls 1–0 at home in Sandy, Utah, a suburb of Salt Lake City.

Confidence also stemmed from the club's belief in relying on its system rather than star players to carry the squad. Each member of the team had a role in helping RSL reach its full potential.

Despite those high hopes, RSL got off to a rocky start in 2009. The club won just three of its first 12 matches. However, all three of those victories were at home, marking

Robbie Findley went on a scoring binge early in the 2009 season.

the start of a season-long trend. Real Salt Lake proved to be nearly invincible at Rio Tinto Stadium, which had opened late in the previous season. In those first three victories, RSL outscored its opponents 12–2. Forward Robbie Findley scored the first hat trick in team history in a 4–1 defeat of the Columbus Crew. He tacked on another goal in a 6–0 blowout of the New England Revolution.

But the early home wins did not translate into momentum for Real. After the New England win, RSL went over a month without posting a single victory.

HOME COOKING, ROAD WOES

Missing the playoffs was a distinct possibility throughout the season. The drastic difference between the team's play on the road—where it won only two matches all season—and at home made it difficult to create and maintain momentum. A road date in mid-June against the mighty LA Galaxy provided the toughest test yet.

LA's roster boasted soccer royalty in David Beckham and Landon Donovan. But star power didn't intimidate RSL, whose team-oriented approach overwhelmed the Galaxy. Forward Yura Movsisyan scored early in the match, and defender Nat Borchers added another goal shortly after halftime.

Yura Movsisyan celebrates his first-half goal in RSL's big victory over the LA Galaxy.

The Galaxy never recovered. Real Salt Lake earned its biggest road win of the season, 2–0 over LA.

The win was proof that Real Salt Lake could match up with the best in a hostile environment. Even though the squad was not known for its star players, RSL's core of Findley, Movsisyan, and defensive midfielder Kyle Beckerman proved the team could compete with anyone. This would be important in the postseason—if RSL got there.

Even after the win against LA, though, Real Salt Lake's play remained inconsistent. It was one step forward, one step back. An example of this frustrating pattern occurred between late June and early August. Real scored seven goals in two convincing home wins against Toronto FC and FC Dallas. But the offense withered on the road. RSL scored only one goal in losses at Columbus and Chicago.

Late in the season, Real Salt Lake found itself in a five-way battle for the final two playoff spots. Heading into the final match of the regular season against the Colorado Rapids, RSL's playoff hopes were on the line.

Led by two first-half goals from Findley and a shutout from goalkeeper Nick Rimando, RSL did its part, blanking the Rapids 3–0 at Rio Tinto Stadium. But the team still needed help to qualify. Three other results broke RSL's way and eliminated teams that were ahead in the standings. Real Salt Lake finished the season with a losing record of 11–12–7 but snuck into the final playoff spot via tiebreaker.

In the regular-season finale, Nat Borchers, *left*, and the RSL defense kept Conor Casey and the Colorado Rapids in check.

WIN OR GO HOME

Real Salt Lake opened the playoffs against Columbus, the defending MLS champions. As was the case earlier in the season against the Galaxy, Salt Lake was not intimidated. RSL beat Columbus 1–0 at home in the first match. But back in Columbus for the second match, the Crew responded by taking a 2–0 lead in the first half. That left RSL behind 2–1 in aggregate. But the match was far from over.

Goals from Javier Morales and Findley within the span of 10 minutes gave RSL a 3–2 lead in aggregate. Midfielder Andy Williams tacked on another goal, and Real Salt Lake moved on to the conference final with a stunning 4–2 win in aggregate over Columbus.

RSL faced the Chicago Fire on the road in a knockout match next. The visitors again were heavy underdogs. In its five years of existence, RSL had only beaten Chicago once. But again, RSL was up to the task. After 120 minutes of defensive struggle, the winner-take-all match went into penalty kicks.

Rimando gave RSL its chance when he stopped Chicago's fourth attempt. Tied 4–4 after five rounds, the shootout went to sudden death. Rimando made two more saves, and RSL finally won when midfielder Ned Grabavoy rifled the ball into

Teammates mob Nick Rimando after the RSL keeper helped the club pull off a playoff upset at Chicago.

the top left corner of the net. Real Salt Lake moved onto the MLS Cup for the first time in franchise history.

STARS vs. SALT LAKE

Eight days later, the team faced its final challenge against the LA Galaxy in one of the most anticipated finals in MLS history. The teams could not have been more different in terms of reputation and tradition. Also, RSL had barely squeezed into

HOME SWEET HOME

Real Salt Lake led MLS with a plus-23 goal differential at home in 2009. In 15 matches at Rio TInto Stadium, RSL won nine, drew five, and lost only one. That was a major reason the team was able to sneak into the postseason.

the playoffs, while all eyes were on LA's star-studded roster. The Galaxy had already won the MLS Cup twice. But this was new territory for Real Salt Lake. Armed with the knowledge that it could beat LA, Real Salt Lake stood tall in a defensive battle in Seattle, the site of that year's final.

RSL frustrated the Galaxy by keeping the ball away from their stars. The teams combined for only seven shots on goal. The score was 1–1 after 120 minutes. Once again, RSL's fate came down to penalty kicks. And again, Rimando played a central role. He stopped one LA shot with a diving save. Then Donovan sent his attempt over the crossbar. RSL led by one after Grabavoy converted in the fourth round. But LA tied it up in the next round when Mike Magee scored and Williams missed.

Each team converted in the sixth round. The pressure continued to build. Now in sudden death, Rimando came up big again. He stopped Edson Buddle's shot to start the seventh round. That left the MLS Cup on the foot of RSL defender Robbie Russell.

Robbie Russell reacts to his title-clinching penalty kick.

The Galaxy's goalkeeper dived to his left as the ball headed toward the opposite corner of the goal. Russell's "Shot Heard 'Round Utah" gave Real Salt Lake a 5–4 victory in penalties and one of the biggest upsets in MLS history. The team with no superstars had earned one of the most unlikely MLS titles in league history.

CHAPTER 2

CLUB
MILESTONES

On July 14, 2004, the course of professional men's soccer in the state of Utah was set. Salt Lake City was awarded an MLS expansion franchise on that day. Up until that point, pro soccer hadn't had much of a presence in the Beehive State. A few minor league teams had come and gone. This would be Utah's first entry in a top-level league.

But it wasn't a complete shock to see Salt Lake City land an MLS team. Utah had developed a strong soccer culture built on youth leagues and tournaments. The state also features a number of popular college teams. When MLS looked to expand for the second time in its brief history, Salt Lake City made a strong bid to earn a franchise.

Real Salt Lake took on the Colorado Rapids in the club's first home match on April 16, 2005.

RSL's name and colors were revealed in October 2004.

    The expansion team was set to join MLS for the 2005 season. But first it needed a name. Ownership decided to call the team Real Salt Lake. The word *real*—pronounced *ray-all*—means "royal" in Spanish. Real Salt Lake was meant as a tribute to classic Spanish clubs such as Real Madrid and Real Betis. The team's main colors, claret and cobalt, were chosen as distinct variations of red and gray, respectively. Although early reactions to the team's name were mixed, the Salt Lake soccer community was excited for play to begin.

John Ellinger was named the first head coach in team history. The team played its first match on April 2, 2005, in New Jersey against the MetroStars. One week later, RSL played its first home match against its new regional rival, the Colorado Rapids. More than 25,000 fans witnessed the team's debut at Rice-Eccles Stadium, home of the University of Utah's football team. Real defender Brian Dunseth's header in the 87th minute gave the home team a 1–0 victory. It was one of the few highlights for the team in the first few seasons, but RSL was slowly building a talented roster.

PUTTING THE PIECES TOGETHER

RSL made a splash before the 2007 season when it traded for goalkeeper Nick Rimando. That year also saw team captain Jason Kreis retire early in the season to replace Ellinger as head coach. The on-field highlight came in the team's first Rocky Mountain Cup win against the Colorado Rapids. RSL stunned its Rocky Mountain rivals 1–0 on a goal from Robbie Findley. That impressive road win at the end of 2007 served as a springboard to 2008.

   The 2008 season was a landmark one for RSL on many fronts. The team opened its brand new soccer-specific stadium in October. Between Rice-Eccles Stadium and Rio Tinto, the

Claret and Cobalt lost only one match in 2008. But they won only two games on the road.

The team did provide one lasting memory away from home. And its timing was perfect. With the team's first playoff spot on the line, RSL paid a visit to rival Colorado on October 25. Colorado scored in the 19th minute, and that lead held up for most of the game. However, RSL's Yura Movsisyan scored off a rebound in the 90th minute, and the match ended 1–1. The draw was enough to knock Colorado out of the playoff race and send RSL into the postseason for the first time in team history.

POSTSEASON RUN

RSL defeated Chivas USA in the opening round of the 2008 playoffs. The team then hosted the conference final against the New York Red Bulls at Rio Tinto Stadium. In the end, RSL lost in bitter fashion, falling 1–0. The rare home loss came at the worst time for the Claret and Cobalt, but still it was a season of firsts.

Along with the first postseason berth, Movsisyan's goal also gave the team its first positive goal differential. Optimism ran high throughout the club after 2008 and led to RSL's memorable run in 2009.

RSL goalkeeper Nick Rimando makes a save in the team's pivotal draw with Colorado in October 2008.

After winning the MLS Cup in 2009, RSL came back strong again the next season. Aside from setting a franchise record for most wins and points in a season, the 2010 squad again was known for its dominance at home. Led by goalkeeper

Nick Rimando and 2010 MLS Defender of the Year Jámison Olave, RSL allowed just 20 goals in 30 matches. That was by far the best mark in the league. The Claret and Cobalt also fielded an explosive offense that scored a league-high 45 goals in 2010. All of this added up to a season in which Real Salt Lake went unbeaten at home. But the season ended with a shocking first-round playoff exit at the hands of FC Dallas.

In 2011 MLS expanded its schedule to 34 matches per team. And over the next four seasons, RSL earned no fewer than 53 points in a season. The team experienced success on several stages of soccer. The 2011 RSL made it all the way to the Concacaf Champions League final before losing to Mexican club Monterrey. In 2012 RSL set franchise records for wins and points but fell to Seattle in its first playoff series. Overall, the team cemented its reputation for home excellence over this span, losing only 12 matches in four seasons. RSL also qualified for the playoffs in seven straight seasons dating back to 2008.

BACK ON TOP

The 2013 season was memorable for RSL from start to finish. A new owner bought the club before the regular season. The club also overhauled its roster by trading a handful of key players, including Olave and midfielder Will Johnson. And it would be

Defender Jámison Olave had a career season for RSL in 2010.

Kreis's final year as head coach. He left after the season to take over an expansion club in New York City.

Still, despite all the changes, RSL reached the US Open Cup final. Then the Claret and Cobalt finished second in the conference with 56 points. After defeating the LA Galaxy and Portland Timbers in the playoffs, RSL earned a spot in its second MLS Cup. The final match against Sporting Kansas City featured two of the smaller cities to host an MLS team. Despite the small-market label, the match for the Cup did not disappoint.

The final went into penalties with the score knotted 1–1 after extra time. RSL lost in heartbreaking fashion, falling 7–6 in the shootout. Despite that disappointment and an early playoff exit the next year, the stretch from 2008 to 2014 represents RSL's finest in franchise history.

The team experienced ups and downs over the next few years. In 2018 and 2019, RSL reached the

UTAH ROYALS FC

In November 2017 RSL acquired the rights to own a franchise in the National Women's Soccer League (NWSL). A club from Kansas City moved to Salt Lake City and became the Utah Royals FC in 2018. The team shared ownership, colors, and a home stadium with RSL. Few teams in the league enjoyed as much support. However, following allegations of racism against the team's owner, he sold the Royals and they moved back to Kansas City.

Midfielder Damir Kreilach scores on a header in the rain to help RSL knock off Portland in the first round of the 2019 playoffs.

playoffs and advanced to the quarterfinals. However, that was followed by a disappointing 2020 season in which the team looked to be back at square one. As it had shown so many times, though, RSL was a team that could never be counted out for long.

CHAPTER 3

STARS OF
SALT LAKE

Forward Jason Kreis became the first Real Salt Lake player after the club acquired him from Dallas. Kreis scored the first goal in franchise history in 2005. Kreis also scored his 100th career goal in 2005, becoming the first player in MLS history to reach the milestone. But his most important contributions to the club came on the sidelines.

Four games into the 2007 season, Kreis retired as a player and took over as coach of RSL. The surprise move came in response to the team's disappointing turn under John Ellinger. Just 34 years old, Kreis was the youngest head coach in league history. A trip to the playoffs in 2008 showed he had the club on the right track.

Jason Kreis is one of the most important figures in franchise history.

Longtime captain Kyle Beckerman also played nearly 60 matches with the US national team.

Kreis's belief in the RSL team-oriented system colored how the squad was built in 2009. With a balanced roster and no superstars, the Claret and Cobalt won their first MLS Cup.

Kreis led the team to the postseason in every year through 2013, including another MLS Cup appearance in 2013. He left RSL after that season as the franchise leader in coaching wins. Kreis was the first of only two players in RSL franchise history whose number was retired.

CAPTAIN KYLE

Defensive midfielder Kyle Beckerman joined RSL in a trade from Colorado midway through the 2007 season. Known for his defensive grit and his ability to start attacks with pinpoint passing, the US national team standout quickly became a team leader for Real Salt Lake. He earned the captain's armband before the 2008 season. He started every match that season, helping the team reach the playoffs for the first time.

In 2009 Beckerman helped the "no-name" RSL squad win the MLS Cup. His leadership and poise in the center of the field helped the team overcome an inconsistent regular season to catch fire in the playoffs. Beckerman became the all-time league leader in appearances by a field player in 2015. Beckerman retired in 2020 following his 14th season with RSL.

The same year RSL got Beckerman, it also traded for forward Robbie Findley. He joined the team from the LA Galaxy. Findley enjoyed a breakout 2009 season when he led the team in goals with 12. The speedy attacker also notched the club's first hat trick in 2009.

Findley is most remembered in RSL lore for scoring the tying goal in the 64th minute of the 2009 MLS Cup. That victory over the Galaxy would not have been possible without Findley's clutch effort.

After leaving Salt Lake City in 2010 to play in England, Findley returned to RSL in 2013 for a second stint. In his return, he came up big once again. Findley scored twice in four postseason starts during RSL's 2013 MLS Cup runner-up finish.

CUNNINGHAM GOES GOLD

Forward Jeff Cunningham had a career year after joining RSL in a trade from Colorado in December 2005. The 29-year-old Jamaican led MLS with 16 goals to earn the Golden Boot. Cunningham was always known as a dynamic scorer, but he put it all together in 2006 with eight assists as well.

SHUTTING THE DOOR

Though he stands just 5-foot-9, Nick Rimando is a towering figure in RSL history. One of the best goalkeepers in MLS history, Rimando joined the club in a trade with DC United in

High-scoring forward Jeff Cunningham won a big award with RSL in 2006.

Nick Rimando was a fixture in the RSL goal for 13 seasons.

December 2006. In a strange twist, Rimando was then traded to the New York Red Bulls on February 9, 2007, only to be traded back two weeks later after RSL keeper Scott Garlick suddenly retired.

Rimando quickly established himself as RSL's top choice in net during the 2007 season. The defense gave up a lot of shots, but he led MLS in saves. His efforts earned him the team Most Valuable Player (MVP) award. In 2008 Rimando picked up where he left off. His stout play in the net carried RSL to a surprising appearance in the conference finals.

The league finally took notice of Rimando in 2009. During RSL's run to the MLS Cup title, Rimando stopped a seemingly countless number of penalty kicks. Highlights included three stops in a shootout victory over Chicago in the conference finals and two more in the shootout against the Galaxy in the MLS Cup. Those moments and more helped make Rimando the 2009 MLS Cup MVP. He was only the second keeper in league history to win that award.

Rimando posted 157 victories in 13 seasons with RSL. He retired from the Claret and Cobalt and MLS after the 2019 season. The six-time All-Star and three-time recipient of the

MLS Save of Year award will long be remembered for his ability to command the game.

MAKING A BIG SPLASH

Costa Rican forward Álvaro Saborío joined RSL on loan from Swiss club FC Sion in 2010. He quickly made a big impact in Salt Lake City, leading the squad with 12 goals in 2010. As a result, Saborío was named 2010 MLS Newcomer of the Year and secured a new four-year contract. He also became RSL's first Designated Player. A Designated Player is usually a star whose contract doesn't count against the league's salary cap.

Saborío played for RSL through 2015 and was a key figure in the team's multiple playoff runs, including the trip to the 2013 MLS Cup. He remains the franchise's all-time leading scorer with 63 goals.

ONLY THE BEST

RSL fans have fond memories of watching Kyle Beckerman, Eddie Pope, and Nick Rimando. Others around MLS took notice, too. In 2020, the league celebrated its 25th season by naming its 25 best players of all time. The three RSL stars were among those included.

Álvaro Saborío drew plenty of attention from opponents when he joined RSL in 2010.

CHAPTER 4

REAL BIG
MOMENTS

The clock was running out on the 2008 season. Real Salt Lake had one last chance to clinch a playoff spot. But it had to go on the road to archrival Colorado, needing at least a draw. And time was literally running out in the match. RSL trailed 1–0 with stoppage time coming up. If the Rapids won, they would be going to the playoffs, and RSL would be out.

RSL tried furiously to score the tying goal. Yura Movsisyan was a good bet to get it. The forward had scored five times in his previous seven league matches. In the 90th minute, RSL had the ball near the penalty area. Robbie Russell used his head to flick the ball into the box. It wound up on the foot of Andy Williams, who was all alone on the keeper.

Yura Movsisyan was part of many big goals for RSL over the years.

Williams took a shot, but the keeper batted it away with his left hand. Fortunately for RSL, Movsisyan was there. He buried the rebound into the empty net. After killing off the final few minutes, RSL celebrated its first-ever playoff berth.

And Movsisyan was not done. He scored the lone goal in a 1–0 win in the first leg of RSL's opening-round playoff series. RSL wound up losing in the conference finals, but it had the makings of an MLS Cup contender. The seeds of the 2009 championship were sown in 2008.

FINDLEY TIES IT UP

Movsisyan does not have the only legendary game-tying goal in Real Salt Lake history. Robbie Findley managed to score an even bigger one. RSL went into the locker room at halftime of the 2009 MLS Cup trailing the LA Galaxy 1–0. Scoring chances became crucial as RSL pushed to tie the match.

In the 64th minute, the ball ricocheted around the Galaxy penalty area. Movsisyan took a shot that was blocked by the legs of a defender. The ball then hit another defender before falling at the feet of Findley. With the keeper scrambling to get back, all Findley had to do was fire it in the gaping net.

Robbie Findley, *left*, and Yura Movsisyan celebrate Findley's tying goal in the second half of the 2009 MLS Cup.

RSL's defense preserved the draw, forcing a penalty kick shootout. Findley converted his chance, and Russell scored the clincher for RSL's first title.

NO PLACE LIKE HOME

FC Dallas knew it had a tough task ahead of it going into the last day of the 2010 season. It faced a road trip to Rio Tinto Stadium, where Real Salt Lake had not lost all season. In fact, RSL had not lost a regular-season match at Rio Tinto since

Álvaro Saborío leaps for a header against FC Dallas in October 2010.

May 16, 2009, a league-record streak of 24 matches. One more win or draw would make RSL the first MLS team to go undefeated at home for an entire season.

The outcome was in doubt until late in the game. The score was 0–0 into the 59th minute. That was when Ned Grabavoy leaped over a Dallas defender to head a ball past the keeper. Javier Morales added a second goal in the 90th minute off a crossing pass from Findley to clinch the win.

RSL went on to run up an unbeaten streak of 37 straight matches across all competitions. Then RSL was stunned on April 27, 2011, in the Concacaf Champions League final. RSL's streak came to an end in a 1–0 loss to Monterrey. RSL's league unbeaten streak ended the next month at 29 matches.

CHAMPIONS LEAGUE SUCCESS

RSL made history in the spring of 2011 when it defeated Costa Rican club Saprissa 3–2 on aggregate in the semifinals of the Concacaf Champions League. That made RSL the first MLS club ever to advance to the final of the regional competition. RSL fell just short in the final, losing on aggregate to Mexican club Monterrey.

OPEN CUP RUN

Rio Tinto was packed on October 1, 2013. The fans were buzzing, hoping to see their team hoist a trophy. In a tough 0–0 battle, the first half was nearly over. But just before the whistle, DC United's Lewis Neal found the back of the net for a 1–0 lead. RSL had to regroup if it wanted to win its first US Open Cup title.

By 2013 the RSL trophy case was still a little empty. But that year, the team had its best-ever run in the US Open Cup. The tournament is a midseason competition that features a knockout format. Clubs from all levels of American soccer play in the competition. It's the oldest national soccer tournament in the country.

RSL had never made the final before. It got to host the match due to the luck of a coin flip. RSL was getting the better chances leading up to Neal's goal. After halftime, RSL was pushing hard. United keeper Bill Hamid was forced to make six saves.

In the 81st minute, leading scorer Álvaro Saborío had a golden chance to tie. One-on-one with Hamid, Saborío fired a shot near the post. Hamid was able to get a hand on it and deflect it away. RSL kept pushing. In stoppage time, a bicycle kick attempt was saved, as was a point-blank shot off a corner kick. Even though RSL had the better chances, United walked away with the trophy. But RSL had another chance at an even bigger trophy later in 2013.

A COLD ENDING

The kickoff temperature of 20 degrees Fahrenheit (minus-6.6°C) made it the coldest match in MLS history. But the frigid weather didn't seem to bother the Sporting KC fans. They packed their home stadium for MLS Cup 2013 and remained loud all day cheering for their team. The cold and the fans made a tough atmosphere for RSL to win its second championship.

After a scoreless first half things began to heat up. Saborío got RSL on the board first, as he had many times before, with

Javier Morales shows disappointment after RSL's bitter defeat in the 2013 US Open Cup final.

a scorching shot past Sporting KC goalie Jimmy Nielsen. RSL narrowly missed chances to double its lead, hitting the post at the 62nd and 73rd minutes. Those chances came back to haunt the Claret and Cobalt as KC scored to tie the match in the 76th minute.

RSL midfielder Ned Grabavoy, *left*, and Sporting KC midfielder Benny Feilhaber battle for the ball during the frigid 2013 MLS Cup.

The score remained tied after two extra periods, sending the match to a penalty shootout. RSL fell behind 2–0, only to tie things up at 3–3 after five rounds. The teams matched each other's hits and misses during the next four turns, making the score 6–6 entering the 10th round of penalty kicks. Finally, Sporting KC won when RSL defender Lovel Palmer sent his kick off the crossbar. Lasting a full 10 rounds, it was the longest shootout in MLS history at the time. But Real Salt Lake had lost out on its second MLS title with yet another shot off the post.

That heartbreaking match would haunt RSL fans for years. It was especially disappointing since the club didn't make it back to the MLS Cup in the years that followed. It even missed the playoffs in two of the next four seasons.

In 2019 the team bounced back. After years of average records, RSL posted the third-best record in the conference and advanced to the conference semifinals. However, a tumultuous year followed. The COVID-19 pandemic disrupted the season. Meanwhile, amid allegations of racism, RSL's owner decided to sell the team. And on top of all that, RSL had one of the worst records in the league. It was a season the team and its fans were ready to put behind them as they sought better days ahead.

TIMELINE

2005 — Real Salt Lake plays its first MLS regular-season game on April 2 in New Jersey against the MetroStars.

2005 — A late header by Brian Dunseth lifts RSL past the Colorado Rapids 1–0 in the club's first home match on April 16.

2008 — RSL opens Rio Tinto Stadium, its new soccer-specific home in suburban Sandy, Utah, on October 9.

2009 — On November 22, RSL wins its first MLS Cup with a dramatic shootout victory over the LA Galaxy.

2011 — Monterrey topples RSL at Rio Tinto 1–0 in the Concacaf Champions League final on April 27.

2012 — Álvaro Saborío sets a club record with 17 goals during the MLS season.

2013 — RSL falls to DC United in the 2013 US Open Cup final on October 1.

2013 — On December 7, RSL loses an epic shootout to Sporting KC in the MLS Cup.

2014 — Longtime RSL goalkeeper Nick Rimando sets the record for the most shutouts in MLS history on August 10.

2019 — Posting their best record in five years, the Claret and Cobalt reach the conference semifinals.

TEAM FACTS

FIRST SEASON
  2005

STADIUMS
  Rice-Eccles Stadium (2005–08)
  Rio Tinto Stadium (2008–)

MLS CUP TITLES
  2009

KEY PLAYERS
  Kyle Beckerman (2007–20)
  Nat Borchers (2008–14)
  Jeff Cunningham (2006–07)
  Robbie Findley (2007–10, 2013–14)
  Jason Kreis (2005–07)
  Jámison Olave (2008–12, 2015–16)
  Nick Rimando (2007–19)
  Álvaro Saborío (2010–15)

KEY COACHES
  Jeff Cassar (2014–17)
  Jason Kreis (2007–13)

MLS DEFENDER OF THE YEAR
  Jámison Olave (2010)

MLS NEWCOMER OF THE YEAR
  Álvaro Saborío (2010)

MLS HUMANITARIAN OF THE YEAR
  Brian Kamler (2005)

MLS ROOKIE OF THE YEAR
  Corey Baird (2018)

MLS SAVE OF THE YEAR
  Nick Rimando (2012, 2013, 2019)

GLOSSARY

aggregate
The combined score of both games in a two-game series.

Designated Player
An MLS player whose salary counts outside the salary cap, allowing teams to sign stars.

draw
A match that ends in a tie.

field player
A player at any position on the field other than goalkeeper.

goal differential
The difference between a team's goals scored and goals allowed.

hat trick
Three goals scored by the same player in one match.

knockout
A kind of competition in which one loss eliminates a team.

leg
One of two matches in a series.

penalty kick
A play in which a shooter faces a goalkeeper alone; it is used to decide tie games or as a result of a foul.

shutout
A match in which a team does not score a goal.

stoppage time
Also known as injury time, a number of minutes tacked onto the end of a half for stoppages that occurred during play from injuries, free kicks, and goals.

MORE INFORMATION

BOOKS

Avise, Jonathan. *Great Soccer Debates*. Minneapolis, MN: Abdo Publishing, 2019.

Marquardt, Meg. *STEM in Soccer*. Minneapolis, MN: Abdo Publishing, 2018.

Marthaler, Jon. *US Men's Professional Soccer*. Minneapolis, MN: Abdo Publishing, 2019.

ONLINE RESOURCES

To learn more about Real Salt Lake, please visit **abdobooklinks.com** or scan this QR code. These links are routinely monitored and updated to provide the most current information available.

INDEX

Beckerman, Kyle, 8, 27–28, 32
Beckham, David, 6
Borchers, Nat, 6
Buddle, Edson, 12

Cunningham, Jeff, 28

Donovan, Landon, 6, 12
Dunseth, Brian, 17

Ellinger, John, 17, 24

Findley, Robbie, 6, 7, 8, 10, 17, 28, 36–38

Garlick, Scott, 31
Grabavoy, Ned, 10, 12, 38

Hamid, Bill, 40

Johnson, Will, 20

Kreis, Jason, 17, 22, 24–26

Magee, Mike, 12
Morales, Javier, 10, 38
Movsisyan, Yura, 6–7, 18, 34–36

Neal, Lewis, 39–40
Nielsen, Jimmy, 41

Olave, Jámison, 20

Palmer, Lovel, 43
Pope, Eddie, 32

Rimando, Nick, 8, 10–11, 12, 17, 20, 28–31, 32
Russell, Robbie, 12–13, 34, 37

Saborío, Álvaro, 32, 40

Williams, Andy, 10, 12, 34–36

ABOUT THE AUTHOR

Sam Moussavi is a novelist and freelance writer based in the San Francisco Bay area. He has written two sets of YA novels as well several nonfiction sports titles.